Meet the Artist

Hilma af Klint

AN ART ACTIVITY BOOK
ANNA DEGNBOL

Visionary

Courageous

Spiritual

Hilma af Klint was born in 1862 into an aristocratic family. She was a visionary abstract artist and spiritualist and is now known as the first person in the world to paint an abstract art work!

She spent the first ten years of her life at Karlsberg Castle, a naval cadet school near Stockholm in Sweden. Her father was a naval commander and taught young sea cadets. He supported af Klint's talents and she was taught mathematics, astronomy and science which was unusual for a girl at the time.

After attending the Royal Academy of Fine Arts in Stockholm, af Klint sold her landscape and portrait paintings to make money. But she was also making radical artworks in a style that had never been seen before! In her lifetime she wasn't very well known and she even requested that her artworks should be kept hidden for twenty years after she died.

It wasn't until recently that the world got to see her extraordinary paintings and now she has rewritten history!

As a child, af Klint spent her summers on an island called Adelsö, in a big lake near Stockholm. It was here that she found a love for nature and science and they became a big inspiration for her.

Her notebooks are full of sketches and studies of plants, flowers, insects and animals. She once even worked as a draughtsman at a vet so that she could study the animals closely! A draughtsman is someone who makes technical and accurate drawings. With practice you can be one too!

Look at this artwork here and see how detailed her drawing is.

Artist's advice
"Every time I succeed in finishing one of my sketches, my understanding of humanity, animals, plants, minerals, of the entire creation becomes clearer."

In the space below, complete the life cycle of the butterfly.

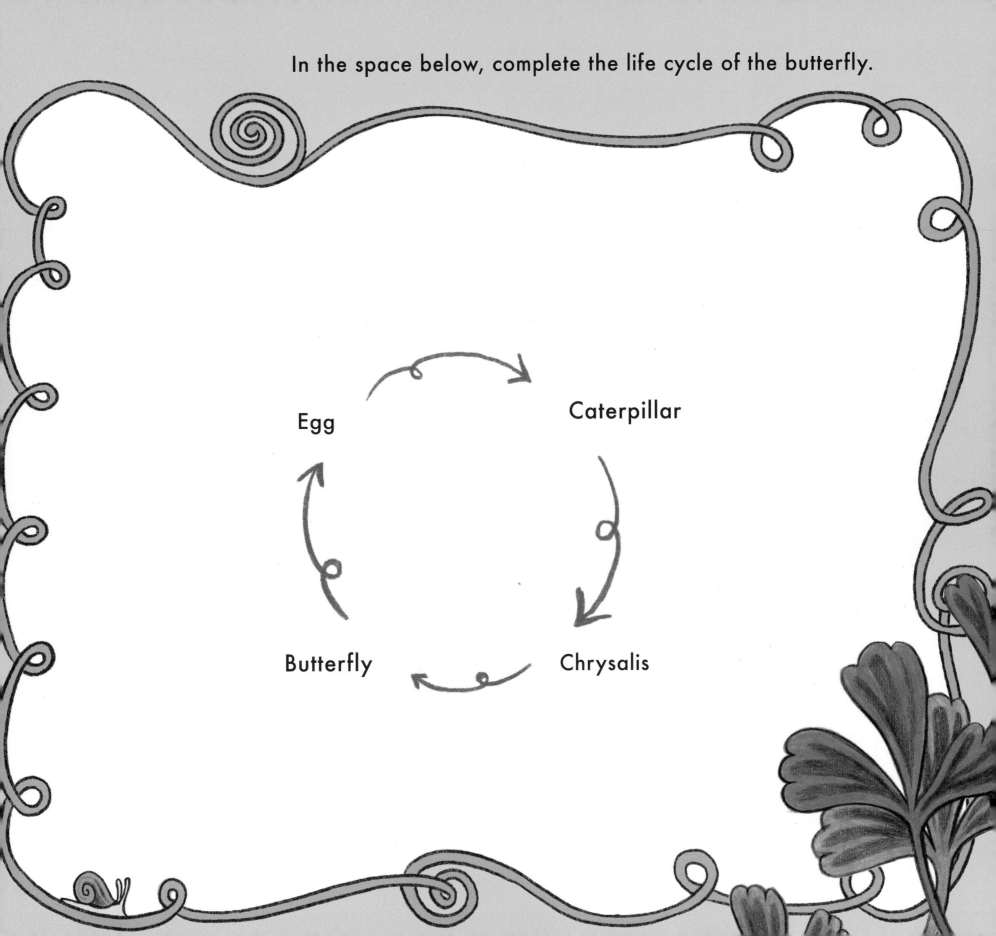

Egg

Caterpillar

Butterfly

Chrysalis

In her notebooks af Klint would paint realistic images of flowers and plants like in this artwork below of some nasturtiums. These are called botanical studies where every detail is recorded perfectly with scientific precision.

Make a pressed flower botanical study!

Top tip! Smaller flowers like daisies are easier to press than big flowers like roses!

You will need:

- Some heavy books or a weight

- Glue

- Some flowers or leaves

- Scissors

- Two sheets of parchment or baking paper

1. Pick some flowers and leaves from your garden. Remember to ask first if it's not your garden!

2. Carefully place the flowers between the two sheets of paper and place it inside one of the books.

3. Stack the other books and weights on top of the book with the flowers inside.

4. Now it's time to be patient and wait 2–3 weeks!

5. Once the wait is over, gently remove the flowers and glue them in this book.

Stick

your

flower

here!

When she was a teenager, af Klint became interested in spiritualism. She wanted to find a way to speak with the invisible spiritual world, and to experiment with new ways of communicating, like using a phone to talk to family and friends

Make your own string phone!

You will need:

2 paper cups

A long piece of string

A sharp pencil

A friend

1. Take your sharp pencil and pierce the bottom of your cup so you have a small hole.

2. Turn your cup upside down and thread your string through the hole and tie a knot at the end so that it can't fall out.

3. Repeat this on your other cup so that the string is attached to both of them.

4. Now go into separate rooms or even outside and try speaking into the cup to send a secret message to your friend. Can you hear them? What does it sound like? How far apart can you stand?

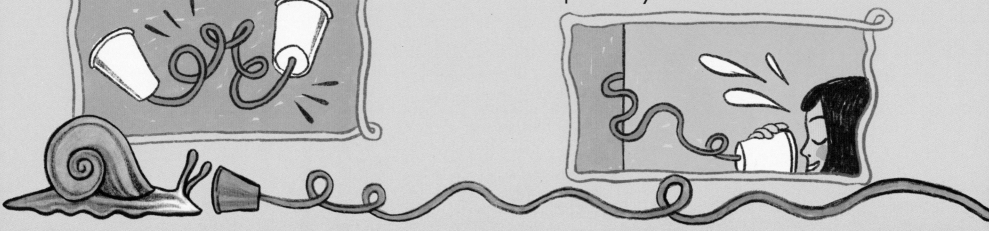

If you could contact another world what message would you leave? Perhaps you have been able to contact an alien or a friend in another dimension? Write them a message here:

For many artists, their dreams were a place of inspiration. When they were sleeping at night they could tune into creative ideas. Af Klint had visions asking her to paint – in 1906 she had one which she called her "great commission" and she spent the next nine years creating a large series called *The Paintings for the Temple*.

Can you remember your dreams? Write them in this dream diary here. Perhaps you'll find inspiration for your next great artwork!

Fun fact! Surrealism explores how our minds work. It's all about our dreams and making art without thinking too hard. So if you doodle when you're daydreaming, then you're probably a surrealist!

In 1896 she started a group called *The Five* with four other women.
They experimented with free flowing or 'automatic' writing and drawings.
The group also liked to make 'exquisite corpse' drawings which was
a way of making an image together as a group.

Make your own exquisite corpse with some friends! You will need:

A friend
(as many as
you like!)
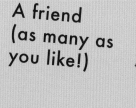

4 pieces
of A4
white paper

Pencils

Sticky tape

1. Tape the short end of the papers together so that you have one long sheet.

2. The first person should take a pencil and draw the head of an imaginary character.

3. Now fold the head over so that it is hidden and pass the paper to your friend.

4. Your friend can now draw the neck and shoulders of your imaginary character.

5. Keep on folding over the paper and drawing the next part of the body until finally you get to the feet.

6. Don't open the sheet of paper until the very end when you can reveal your character!

Over 100 years after Hilma af Klint had dreams about her paintings, artists in the 1960s made a machine to help people enter their dreams even if they were awake!

They called it the Dreamachine! The patterns and shapes were supposed to create a relaxed mood and help them find artistic vision!

Top tip! Close your eyes and let your imagination be your guide!

Create your own Dreamachine lightshade and enter into a magical dream world to discover your inner creative side!

You will need:

A3 piece of paper or card

Scissors

Sticky tape

Coloured tissue paper

A lamp or lightbulb

1. Copy or trace the shapes below onto your piece of card using your pencil.

2. Make sure to cover the entire page but leave gaps in-between the shapes.

3. With the help of an adult, take the scissors and cut out these shapes so you are left with a stencil shape.

4. Stick pieces of coloured tissue paper over the holes.

5. Bend the paper so that it forms a conical shape like a tube and tape the sides together.

6. Place the tube over a lamp or light bulb with the help of an adult.

7. Now turn off all the other lights and let the shapes and colours dance across your room!

In 1906 af Klint's style changed and she began to make radically abstract paintings – unlike anything that had been made before. They were bold and colourful and used unusual shapes, swirls and patterns.

Hilma af Klint used something called tempera to paint with, a mixture of egg yolk and pigment.

Have you painted with an unusual mixture before? Have you ever tried painting with bubbles?

Her series *The Paintings for the Temple* is huge! It has 193 artworks and they are massive in size! The painting above is three metres high — much taller than anyone you know!

Make your own bubble painting!

You will need:

Washing up liquid

A straw

Paper

Cups

Water

Coloured craft paints

1. In your cups, mix a few drops of paint with washing up liquid and half a cup of water together.

2. Use a straw to blow into the mixture to create lots of bubbles. You want the bubbles to almost spill over the top!

3. Gently place a piece of paper over the bubbles. The bubbles will burst but they are meant to!

4. Remove the paper to see the pattern underneath. Let it dry then repeat!

The nineteenth century was full of scientific inventions and discoveries which blurred the lines between art, science and reality. Things that were once invisible could be seen for the first time, for example radiation waves. Normally, artists tried to show the real world as they saw it around them, but af Klint tried to paint the invisible world that we can't see.

Can you draw what you think these waves and rays look like?
Use your imagination and don't worry, it doesn't have to be accurate!

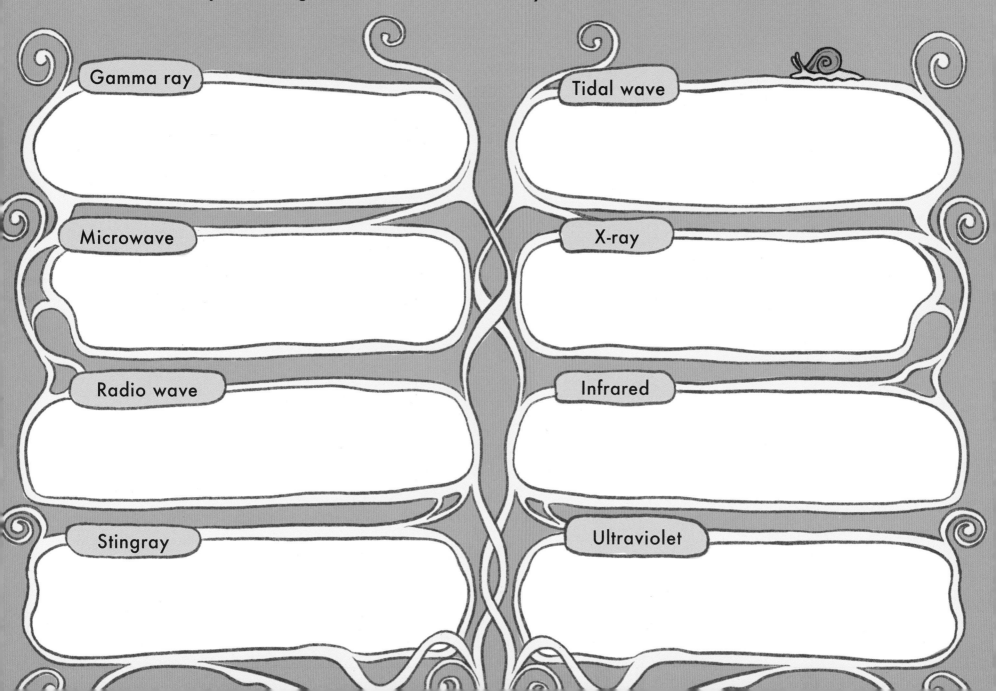

Gamma ray

Tidal wave

Microwave

X-ray

Radio wave

Infrared

Stingray

Ultraviolet

Lots of af Klint's work involved symmetry like this painting.
Hold a mirror in the centre of this work. Is it perfectly reflected?

Place a piece of paper on the other side of your mirror.
Can you copy the work accurately?

Hilma af Klint's artworks are inspired by science, magic and botany like this painting called *The Tree of Knowledge*.

She was interested in the discovery of the atom, the smallest particle in the world which makes up everything we see around us. Lots of her artworks show spirals and orbiting shapes like tiny atoms or cosmic planets out in space.

Make your own cosmic DIY Spirograph drawing!

You will need:

Pencil

Scissors

PVA glue

Bowl

Thick cardboard (with corrugated strips in the middle of the sheet)

Mug

Hole puncher

Coloured ballpoint pens

1. Take your thick cardboard and trace around the bowl with the pencil (roughly 15cm in diameter) to create a circle.

2. With the help of an adult cut out the circle so that you have a circle shaped hole in the cardboard.

3. Cut a long strip of cardboard, about 45cm long and 2cm wide.

4. Peel off the top layer of this strip so you reveal the corrugated (bumpy) layer underneath.

5. Put a thin layer of PVA glue on the flat side of this strip and gently stick it to the inside of your circle so the ridges face inwards.

6. Using the mug as a guide, draw a smaller circle on a new piece of cardboard and cut this out to create a disk.

7. Punch some random holes into this disk using the hole puncher.

8. Cut another, smaller strip of cardboard out and glue this to the outside on the disk so the ridges face outwards.

9. Place a sheet of paper under the cut-out circle and put your disk on top. Hold a pen through the hole and use it to drag the disk around the edge of the inner circle. The disk should start to revolve, fitting within the bumps of the outer circle like a cog.

10. Go around the circle a few times and see your pattern start to emerge, you can experiment by punching the holes in different places and with different coloured pens!

Hilma af Klint was a vegetarian and loved animals and plants.

One particular animal that appears a lot in her work is a snail. She believed that snails had magical properties because they were hermaphrodites which mean they are both male and female. They also have a spiral shell which had a powerful meaning for her. It represented evolution as the spiral pattern swirls both inwards and outwards.

Colour in these shells.
Can you spot who
might be living
in them?

How many
snails can you
find in this book?

Hilma af Klint had lots of ideas about the universe and the world. She could see how everything was connected from the smallest atom to the largest star out in space. She was very spiritual and was interested in Theosophy, a special kind of religion inspired by Buddhism, Hinduism and ancient Greek Philosophy. Theosophy was based on mysticism, which is the belief that there is a whole other world, beyond what we can see in the visible world around us. Some people could experience this world through meditation or like af Klint, through her dreams.

Can you help af Klint travel across this imaginary universe to find her snail?

Theosophy taught that different colours have different meanings and can make you feel certain ways.

What colours would you use to express these feelings and moods? Draw a face here to express that emotion using only one colour.

Embarrassed

Shy

Angry

Excited

Thoughtful

Tired

Sad

Happy

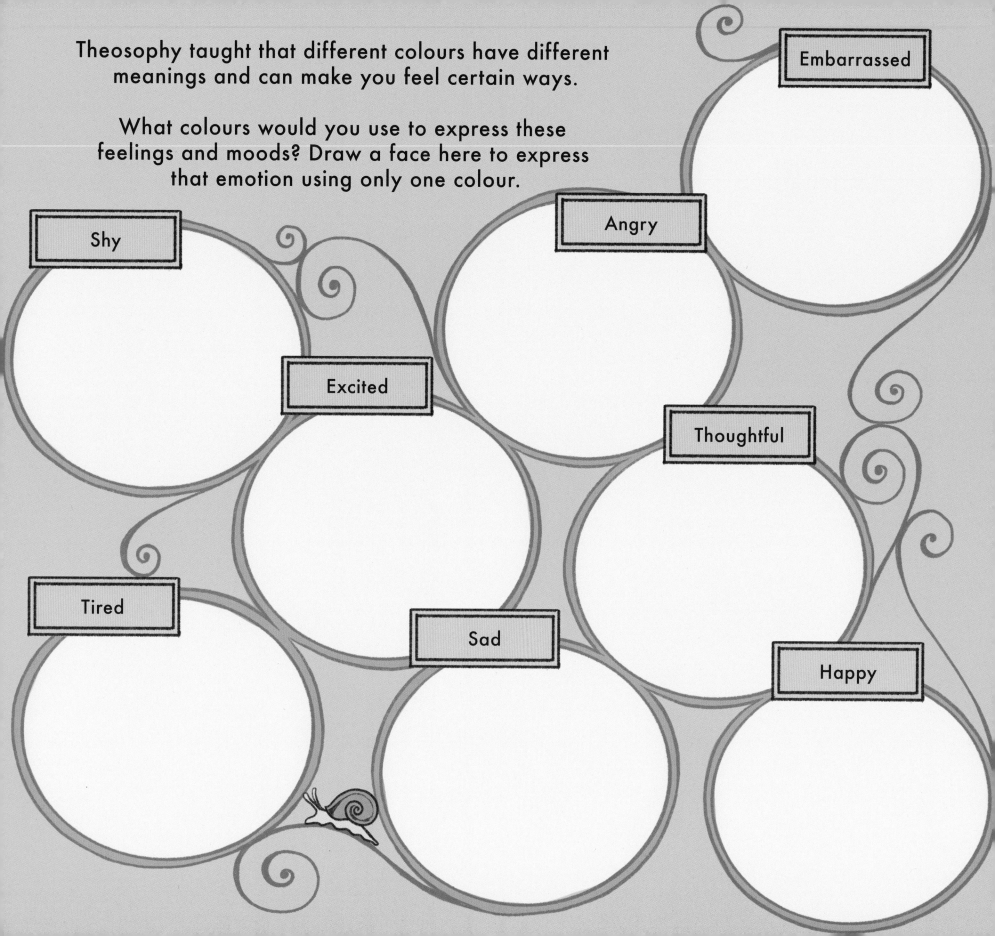

Discover the magic of light with your own colour prism!

You will need:

A glass of water

A torch

White paper

A small hand mirror

A dark room

1. Fill the glass with water and put it on a table.

2. Place the mirror inside the glass at an angle.

3. Turn on your torch and then turn off the lights and close the curtains.

4. Aim the torch light at the mirror and watch the magical light display!

Hilma af Klint used lots of geometric shapes but also squiggles, swirls, blobs and other unusual shapes in her art.

She sometimes tried 'automatic drawing' to explore the world in her mind.

Make your own automatic drawing in the space opposite!

Grab a pencil, shake your arms out and take two deep breaths. Now close your eyes and without taking the pencil off the page, draw randomly, without thinking about it too much. You could even experiment by using the hand you don't normally write with. What can you see in your drawing and what does it mean?

Hilma af Klint used lots of symbols and colours, each with different meanings. Some of them we can understand and some are still a mystery!

This artwork is a study on cereal oats!

What kind of breakfast do you have?

Draw it here.

In the grid below come up with your own secret language using shapes, patterns, words and colours.

After many years of her work being kept secret, we can now see what a truly extraordinary, brave and visionary artist Hilma af Klint was, and there are still many more secrets of hers to discover!

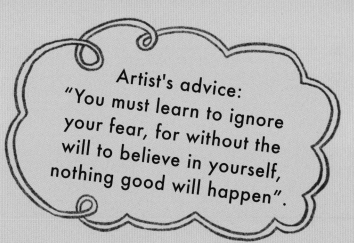

Artist's advice: "You must learn to ignore your fear, for without the will to believe in yourself, nothing good will happen".

Aa	Bb	Cc	Dd	Ee	Ff	Gg
Hh	Ii	Jj	Kk	Ll	Mm	Nn
Oo	Pp	Qq	Rr	Ss	Tt	Uu
Vv	Ww	Xx	Yy	Zz	!	?

Page 4:
Apple undated
Watercolour on paper
16 × 14.5
The Hilma af Klint
Foundation

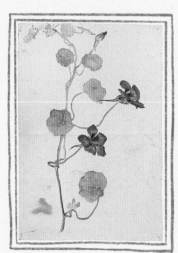

Page 6:
Nasturtium
c. 1890
Watercolour and ink on paper
23.5 × 35
The Hilma af Klint
Foundation

Page 20:
*The Swan, No.19, The SUW
Series, Group IX: Part I*
1914–15
Oil paint on canvas
148.5 × 152
The Hilma af Klint
Foundation

Page 17:
*The Evolution, No.6, The WUS/Seven-
Pointed Star Series, Group VI* 1908
Oil paint on canvas
100.5 × 132.5
The Hilma af Klint Foundation

Page 14:
The Ten Largest, No.3, Youth, Group IV
1907
Tempera on paper, mounted on canvas
321 × 240
The Hilma af Klint Foundation

Page 18:
Tree of Knowledge, No.5
The W Series 1915
Watercolour, gouache,
graphite and ink on paper
45.8 × 29.5
The Hilma af Klint
Foundation

Page 26:
The Eros Series, No.6, The
WU/Rose Series, Group II
1907
Oil paint on canvas
58 × 79
The Hilma af Klint
Foundation

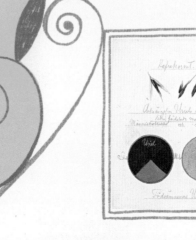

Page 26:
A Work on Cereals, Oats
16 August 1920
Watercolour, graphite and
metallic paint on paper
15 × 12
The Hilma af Klint
Foundation

First published 2023 by order of the Tate Trustees
by Tate Publishing, a division of Tate Enterprises Ltd,
Millbank, London SW1P 4RG
www.tate.org.uk/publishing

Illustrations © Anna Degnbol 2023

Photo credits:
All works © Jessica Höglund, The Hilma af Klint Foundation

A catalogue record for this book is available from the British Library

ISBN 978 1 84976 846 7

Distributed in the United States and Canada by ABRAMS, New York
Library of Congress Control Number applied for

Colour reproduction by DL Imaging, London
Printed and bound by Litografia Rosés / SYL L'Art Grafic, Spain

Measurements of artworks are given in centimetres, height before width